Funky Art & Fun for Everyone

Whirled Wide Designs

Sheila Leigh Williams

Tellwell Talent
www.tellwell.ca

ISBN
978-0-2288-0202-0 (Paperback)

TOP 10 THINGS
THAT MAKE THIS BOOK *AWESOME*

10. Play involving mind & colours helps balance toxic-overburden. This book provides a perfect organic break from screens & today's general rediculality.

9. Only basic Art kit supplies are needed to create projects – no noise toys required.

8. It saves $$ for its users with pages of 1-of-a-Kind greeting card & gift materials.

7. Perfection is Not a priority – Dedication to the project is. ***Completion feels good.***

6. The challenges are good for **all ages** provided someone with scissor skills is helping.

5. Random Colour challenges ***dare*** your authentic self ***to accept*** what magic can bring ....a test of the acceptance of what is - only good

4. Funky terrain of the art in this book encourages others to follow their own natural style, as did the author (like seriously - i can barely draw a stick-man! if I can 'do art' then You can too!)

3. Spend Time Not $$- Take it to places of quiet where creating can be part of the learning & healing, like escapes away from $$ zones – where Time is your friend.

2. Less is More - Use This book !! wrapping, gifts, race tracks, puzzles, challenges - Enough variety for everyone in the room to find a project. Simple is great.

1. No Pressure -This book will be waiting for a time when you get to relax your body & PLAY with colourful projects that can free your mind & feed your soul.

Take Time – Make a Mess – Have Fun
(Having fun Helps!)

Playing (in any way) keeps us Friendly
Friendly = Bonding
Bonding = Trust
Trust = Opens opportunities for release through colour, play & creation
of all kinds.

~~~~~~

Remember

***You are Safe within the pages of this book ***

It is a gift ~
I made it for you...

InJOy

~~~~~~

Sheila Leigh Williams - whirledwidedesigns.com

RANDOM COLOR SELECT

*Sometimes its Fun to Play with colours in
different ways than they "should be"*

Object

To assign colours to the *Symbols of a colouring page by random selection & to **challenge** the self to go with the colours that the random colour select challenges you with. Black & White should Not be included in the random colour picks

*letters, stars, fish, circles, bones etc.

What is Important is that **All of 1 kind of Symbol has All the same colour**

** The background area can also be assigned a colour

Instructions

Removing the page from the book to work on it is optional
1. Pick a page to colour then write down a list of all the symbols on that page.
2. Write 10-12 colours you have to work with onto small pieces of paper of equal size.
3. Fold those papers & put them into a bag so that someone can pull one at a time to determine which colour will go to which symbol., remove the colour from choices once selected

4. pull the folded papers out 1 at a time writ the selected colour beside the symbol. Work down from the top of the list until each symbol has a colour assigned to it – any variation of that colour is allowed to be used.
5. Colour & see what happens!

Hands + Heart = Art - Just add colours!

SPEED MAZES

2 WAY SPEED RACES

<u>There are 3 - 2 Way Speed Maze race tracks in this book to Finger race on</u>

Object

To be the 1st Finger racer to reach the "Home Base" (starting point) of the other player across the maze without lifting a finger & having to start again.

Instructions – removing the track from the book is optional
1. Each player chooses a side for their Home Base to start from
2. After the 1st race the players SWITCH Home Bases & race Again repeating step 4.

*There will be a total of 4 races meaning each players races from each side twice

To Begin:
3. The 2 players place their fastest racing fingertip on one of the 2 starting ends of the track – *use the Non racing hands to hold the track down while racing
4. ALL racers COUNT ALOUD TOGETHER AS THEY RACE beginning with a 1-2-3 GO -**Fingertips Must remain ON the track for the entire race!** if lifted from the track that player must return to their home base **& begin again.**

   *Counting Together **continues** until All racers make it to their destinations at the other players Home Base **OR** in the Infinity Races, back to their own home bases.

**The count when they reach home base is their 'time' for that race even if they had to start again & counting continues until they are home.

5. Racers take note of EACH race time count then ADD ALL 4 races totals together

The Finger racer with the **LOWEST combined times** of the 4 races **WINS!**

~~~~~~

INFINITY SPEED RACES
<u>There are 2 computer drawn infinity mazes in this book</u>

Object
To be the 1st Finger racer to complete a **full loop** & return to chosen their Home Base.

Instructions
1. Up to 4 players begin by each placing a fingertip at different places around the outside of the maze -This will become their HOME BASE.
2. Racers will use one hands fingertip for racing & the other hands fingertip to mark their Home Base, beginning & ending the race at the same spot – fingers **stay on the track** until everyone finishes the race by getting back to their own Home Bases.

To Begin:
3. Follow the same instructions as 2 Way Speed #2 - Together 1-2-3... where
4. *AS ABOVE All players must Continue to COUNT TOGETHER ALOUD until All racers that are left racing make it back home.

- ADD the race times together & the Finger racer with the LOWEST NUMBER **WINS!**
~~~~~~

3 PAGE - 4 PIECE PUZZLES

Instructions
1. Find the 3 pages in the book with the 4 mixed images on each & remove all gently from the book.
2. VERY CAREFULLY CUT with scissors along the DOTTED lines that run through the middle of the puzzle pieces on each page to leave 12 small pieces total.
3. Cut off all excess white edge paper beyond the border line that matches up around the edges of each full puzzle – not all puzzle pieces are the same size and some are just funky

At this point the Options are:
Use in a Random Colour Select Challenge –
or - Have you and 11 of your friends colour them all at once and assemble when done
or - Pick 1 puzzle for you & your friends to work on first
or - Gather all 12 of the uncoloured pieces into a funky mini book & gift it to a friend

Then - Carefully assemble the COLOURED puzzle pieces & paste with glue stick or what have you, onto a white or coloured background piece of paper of your choice
-You can frame these masterpieces & hang them up, use for a greeting cards or a gift them to friends!

ART is FROM the HEART - GIFT IT to a FRIEND

...because it's like giving Gold to the Soul

MAKE YOUR OWN GREETING CARDS

This book is a **resource of Art supply** for those who like to save $$ and make their own One-of-a-Kind greeting cards for friends and family events.

Provided
Are 3 pages of slogans & 2 pages of borders to cut out & paste together to make your special card. Use anything you want to- magazine pics etc. also work - search for extra borders throughout this book or others! *Everything is Art Supply!*

There are also 3 other pages with the large words FEEL; GIVE; & PLAY in the centre of them – parts of these page can also be coloured, cut & pasted to make many variety of greeting cards.

~~~~~~

Object
To save $$ and make something special for someone special on their special day

Instructions
1. Find any sized strong paper, like construction paper & FOLD IT in HALF to look like a book.
2. DECIDE what the theme of your card will be & choose from the book the best slogans & adornments you would like to put on the front of the card. You can always add your own too!
3. COLOUR any adornments & borders you choose BEFORE cutting from pages to paste onto the card.
~~~~~~

4. CENTRE the Main phrase on the front of the card with all slogans of borders that you wish to use around it before pasting anything down – make sure you like your design before you paste it down. Play with all pieces until it works.
5. When ready, paste words & adornments down with glue stick or what have you.
6. WRITE something personal on the INSIDE of the card to the special person – Adding a second page with more adornments inside is also nice – **Improvise!**

Tips

-You can use any variety of pens, pencils, paints or pictures to add to you card – just give yourself PLENTY OF TIME to make it – Days before the day of the event is Always Best!

-Feel free to glue ribbons & add sparkles or fabric, stickers, toys, etc. to enhance overall look to the card – **Be Creative...it's your Gift!**

NEVER be afraid of Perfection – **Art does Not demand** it of you – if you Made it (even funky) then it is Already perfect because it was Made by YOU with a **focus & love...**

***PLEASE **ALWAYS** Remember to Be VERY Careful when using scissors - if too tricky get someone more able TO HELP you cut them out

ALWAYS SAFETY FIRST !!

4 PAGE JUMBO PUZZLE SEARCH

There are 4 pages in this book **that go together** to create **1 Jumbo** picture.

Directions

1. Find the pages that go together and remove them carefully from the book.
    ***It's recommended to colour BEFORE mounting** depending on how you plan to adhere onto a larger backdrop.
2. This will require a large piece of paper or cardboard to mount the 4 page puzzle pieces onto – carefully put the 4 pages together & trim any excess edges until all 4 pages fit seamlessly together.
3. Next (once coloured) carefully place the pages together then flip all upside down to share a vertical piece of clear packing tape that will run along the seams – (desk tape works as well).

This tape will be ON THE BACKSIDE of the pages

4. – after taped together, carefully adding a layer of clear packing tape across entire 4 page front makes it firmer to hang as well as somewhat waterproof. Your choice.

SEEK A WORD OR PHRASE

There are **3 traditional** SEEK A WORD puzzles to solve in this book...
...and UN-traditionally, NO solutions will be given! You must find all the words on the list on your own...because sometimes life is like that!

*Yes all the words are in there! - ***Always keep seeking solutions!***

Object
To find all the words in the lists below the centre square of funky letters

Instructions
All words in the lists are found going in All Directions, up, down, across & diagonal in a straight line

1. Carefully circle the words so as to still see the letters, some of which are reused
2. Once you find the word cross it off the list so you know its gone

Options
-Timing oneself from start to finish
-2 can race each other on different puzzles

*Borders of finished puzzles can be used as borders for Greeting Cards – **Reuse this book!**

There are **6 SEEK A PHRASE** pages in this book

Object

Use the small hint words to figure out the best phrase made out of the funky jumbled letter maddness

Instructions

1. Write down ALL the words you can create with the random letters on the page
2. See who can find the phrase first...or not ***just have fun with it!***

Options

These Pages can be used in the RANDOM COLOUR CHALLENGE

*This is when colours are randomly selected for each of the letters or shapes in the chosen page – the selected colours (or versions of) then go to each of the diff shapes/letters & backspace - Let **Randomness** decide for you today

Expand your Norms – Try a Random Colour Challenge!

MANDALA CHALLENGE

Mandala -The Definition – "A symbol in a dream representing the Universe in Hindu & Buddhist symbolism"

Today its cross cultural significance is to represent the Universe...and what some (like me) would perceive as the Inner Verse

*When you set about to create a Mandala you have really begun a small journey to self enrichment. *Everything* that it takes to make a mandala *is what you will need in life* to cope with ongoing challenges. Enter the inner world to see your balance on paper.

By taking the time for a MANDALA CHALLENGE you will be entering a zone where many decisions have to be made. Time is needed to honour its potential to be completed. Without realizing it you will be cultivating **excellent** personal traits that will become ever employable Mental Tools to add to your personal mental tool kits – traits such as: CONSISTANCY, BALANCE, SIMPLICITY, CONNECTION, PERSERVERANCE, CENTEREDNESS, INNER BEAUTY, RELEASE.... and most importantly CALM

sooo crucial for today's sanity levels.

~Others have said that Mandalas in dreams represent the dreamers search for completeness & self-unity~

Making a mandala doesn't have to *mean* anything. Completing the piece to the edge Does!

Adding colours to your mandala is optional...

...however when coloured they make great small Wrapping paper or Greeting card material!

Pssssst -**Spend Time not $$**

Provided - A dark lined Grid is provided with Pre-set equal points around the centre to help navigate a pattern. Using these is Not mandatory – its all up to you!

Object
To keep adornments around the centre point equal on all sides & lines as straight or similar to the other sides as possible...then take time to finish it to the edge.

Instructions
1. Find a blank white sheet of paper to fit over top of the Pre-made Grid & attach to the grid sheet with **paper clips** on each corner – **or** to a **clipboard** if you have one
2. Rulers are optional – Don't be bullied by perfection - ***Enjoy the challenge!!***

MANDALA GRID

This is for **UNDER** another sheet of blank paper
DO NOT DRAW ON THIS SHEET!!

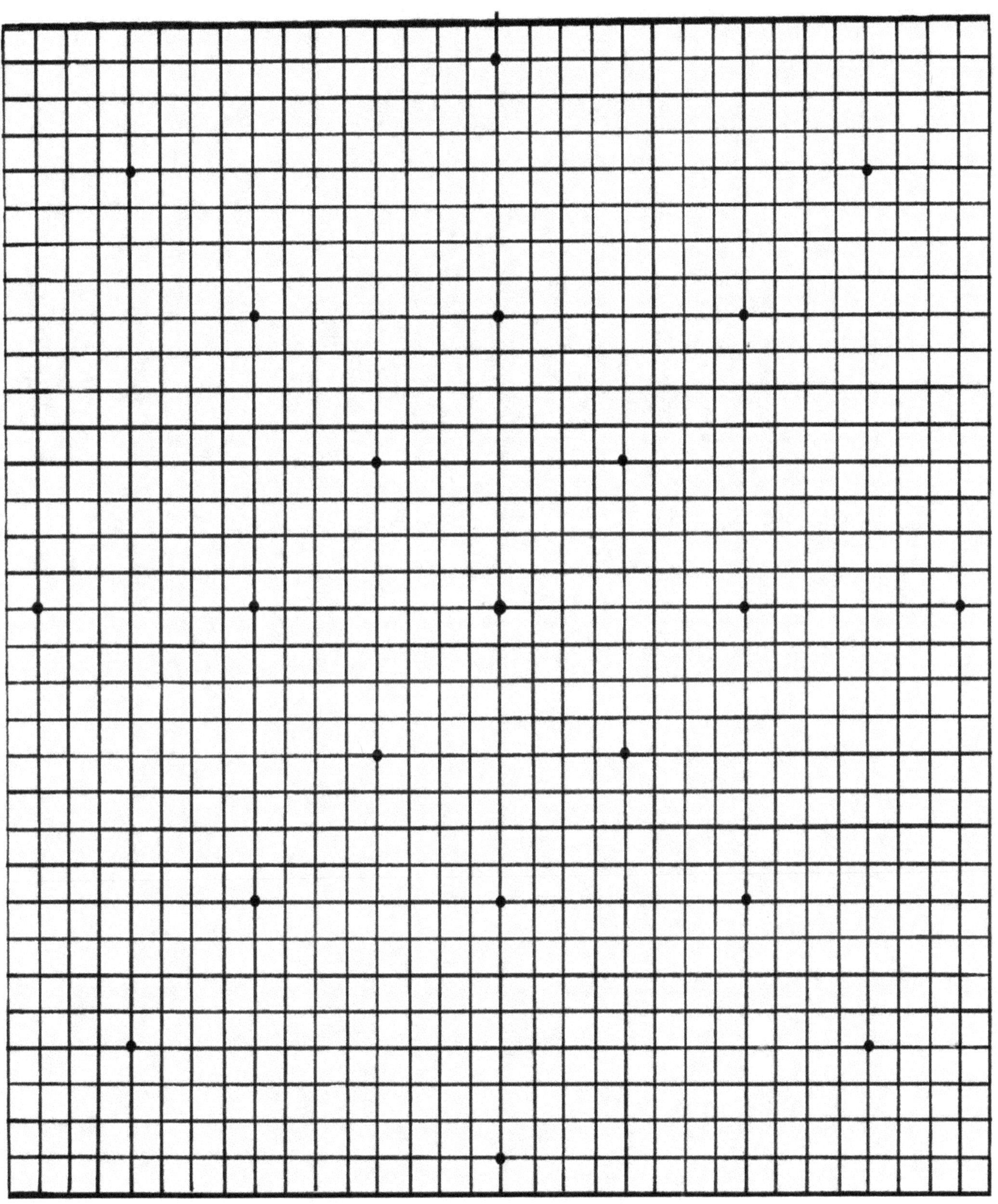

RELAX

```
P T F R U N N I N G A H S E L I M S
A S G I E I P L I S T E N M E O P E
S E A E R N B R R L N J O M U S T N
S U R E N E A E A S O L I N K S E I
G G D P E I C E E Y E P T L Z A I L
N P E R S N H S L T I A A O E L U C
O T N D A N Z S O C I W C G A G Q E
S Y A D I L O H N N R E A C H N M R
D O Q T O K D I T U A S V C O I O E
R G L U H R C O T N S N R R T P S R
I A N A I G P O B A O O I Y U M D O
B G Q V R T I R M W T S S P U A H H
E E E A A N E L O M K I P R E C W S
I S Z O N E A R E B A Y D R A E O A
N E L E Z C K S E D I H T E M P L E
G F R E S E M O H E L I B O M O S S
```

AGES
BACH
BEACH
BEER
BEING
BIRD SONGS
CALM
CAMPING
CLEANER
DAISYTIME
DANCERS
DELIGHT
DRIVES
DRUMS
ENJOY
FIRE
FLOAT

GARDEN
GLASS
GRAZE
GREEN
GUEST
HAMMOCK
HEALTH
HIDES
HOLIDAYS
HOMES
HOTEL
INNER
LISTEN
LOUNGE
MASSAGE
MEDITATION
MOBILE HOME

MOSS
MOUNTAIN TOP
MUSIC
MUST
NO RISK
NO WORK
OCEAN BREEZE
ORDER IN
PASS
PETS
PICNIC
POEM
PRAY
PUPPY
QUIET
QUIT
REACH

READ
RECLINE
ROADS
RUNNING
SEA SHORE
SENSES
SHAG
SLEEP IN
SLOW
SMILES
SOLAR
SUNSHINE
TEMPLE
TORCH
VACATION
WALKS
YOGA

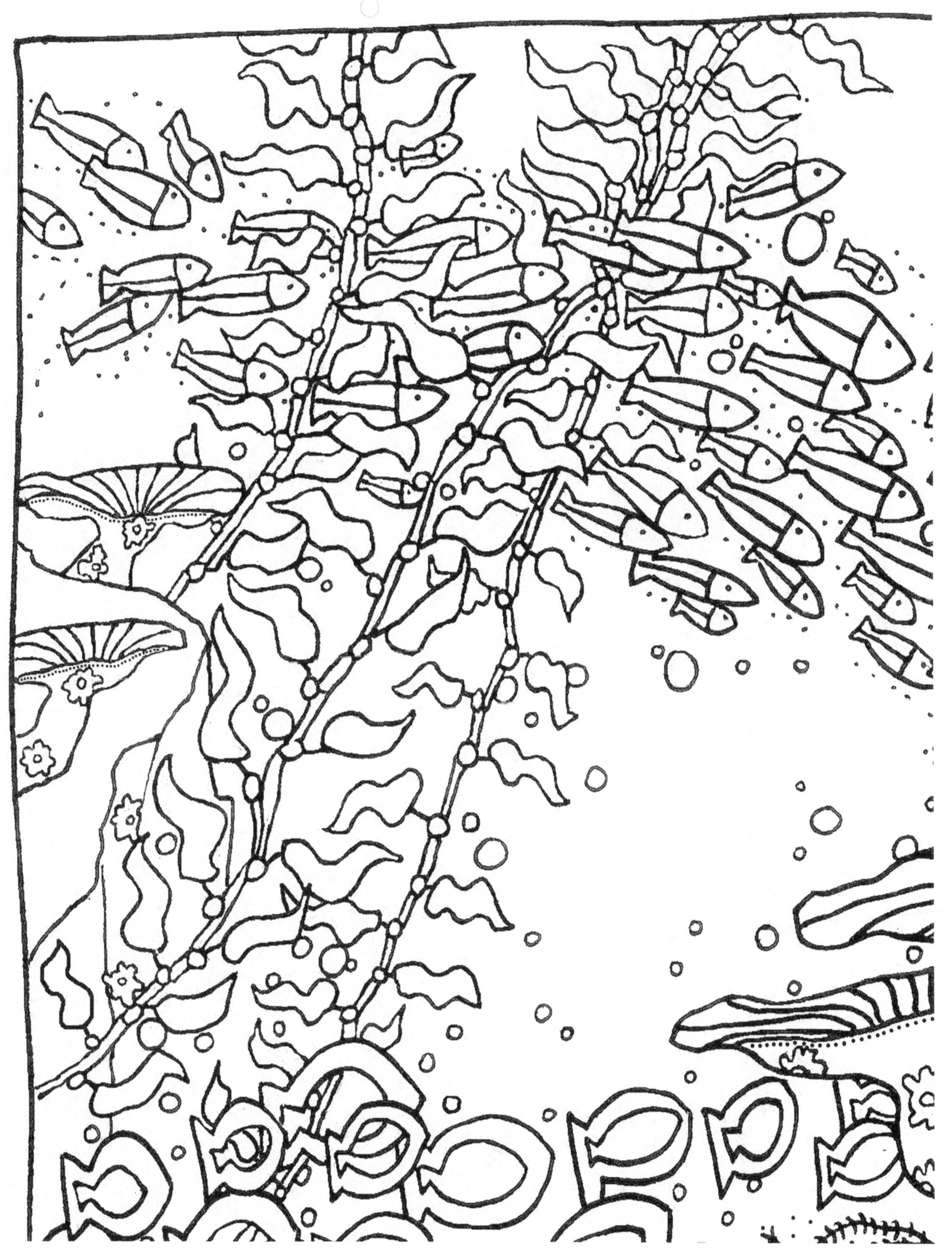

BALL
STEREO
REAL
MUSIC
FREE
GOLF
CARDS
OFTEN
GAMES
catch
together
NICE
SAFE
hard
TRUE
FAIR
Lottery
AWARE
Time
NOW
CALM
proud
PLAY

to LAUGH · Your Day

LAUGH · THE BEST

U ROK · good luck

AWESOME · Happy YOU Day!

Thank You! · LAUGH

ALL GOOD

SOO FINE · have a · SPECIAL

GO For It! · It's ALL GOOD

2 WAY SPEED RACE #1

51

happy
safe
Loved
ALiVE
Pride
PEACE
Sunshine
warm
OPEN
CALM
FEEL
READY
energy
Pain
OK
WiLD
GOOD
STRONG
RAin
FREE
AWAKE
Able
worthy
WELL
Joy

BEACH

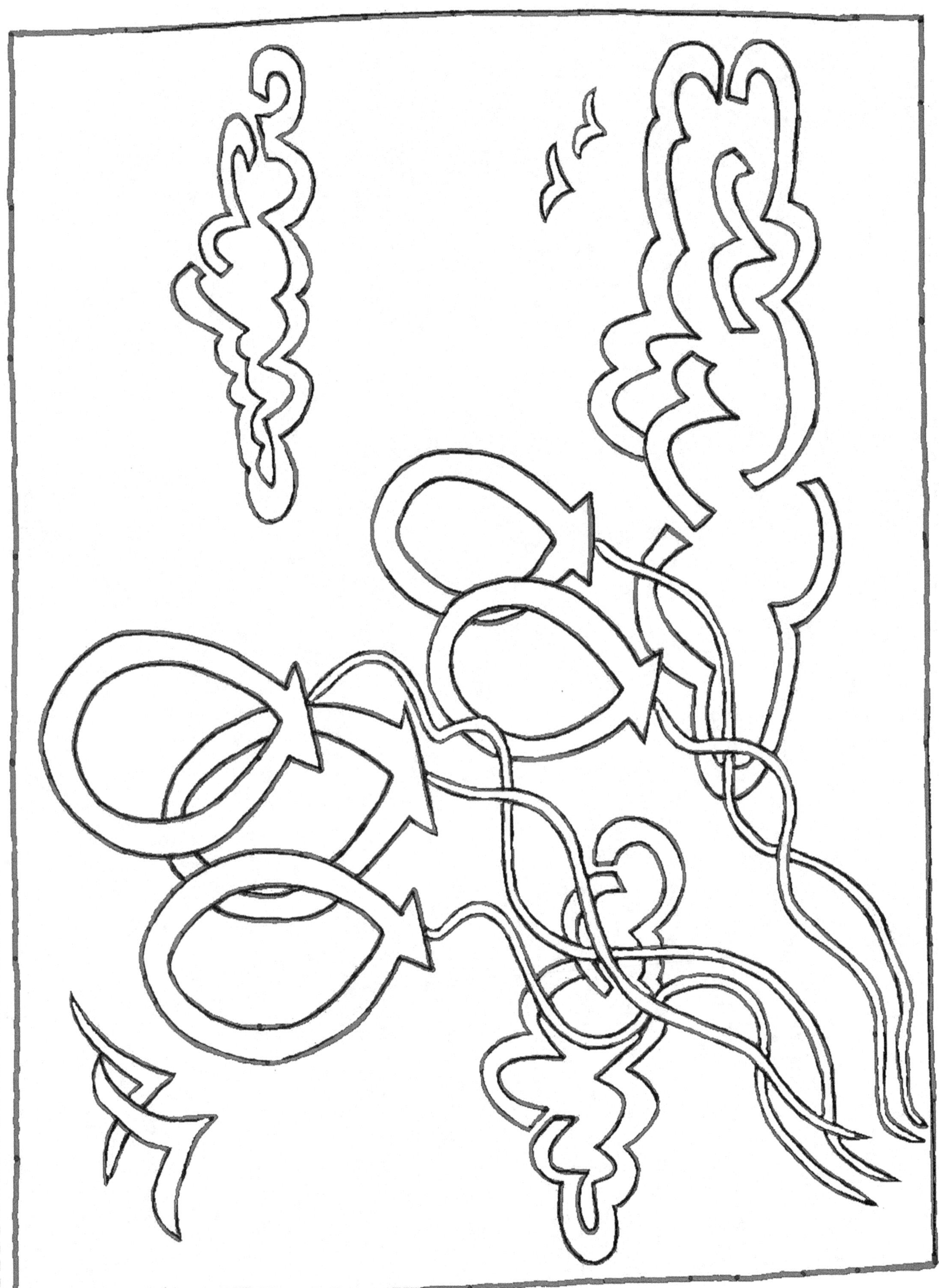

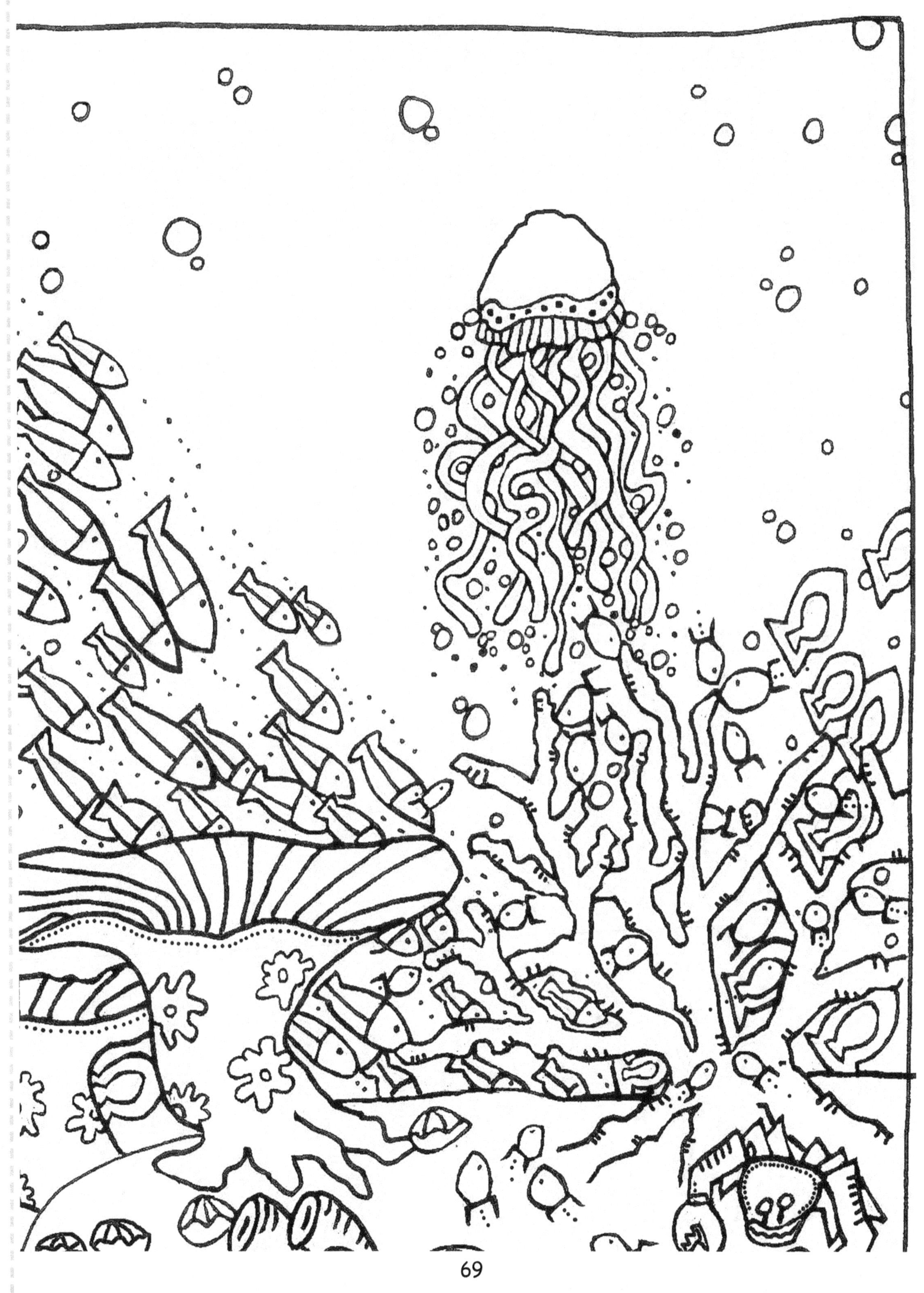

Change is · <u>HAPPY EVERYDAY</u>

somtimes · we R · we can · be Great

TOO FAR · MY♡ · FORWARD

Happy Every Day! · AWESOME

WE ♡ YOU · Is GOOD · YES ·

GET WELL SOON · better · Anytime!

Cheers · GOOD LUCK

GOOD LUCK · it's TIME

Thank you · THANK YOU So much

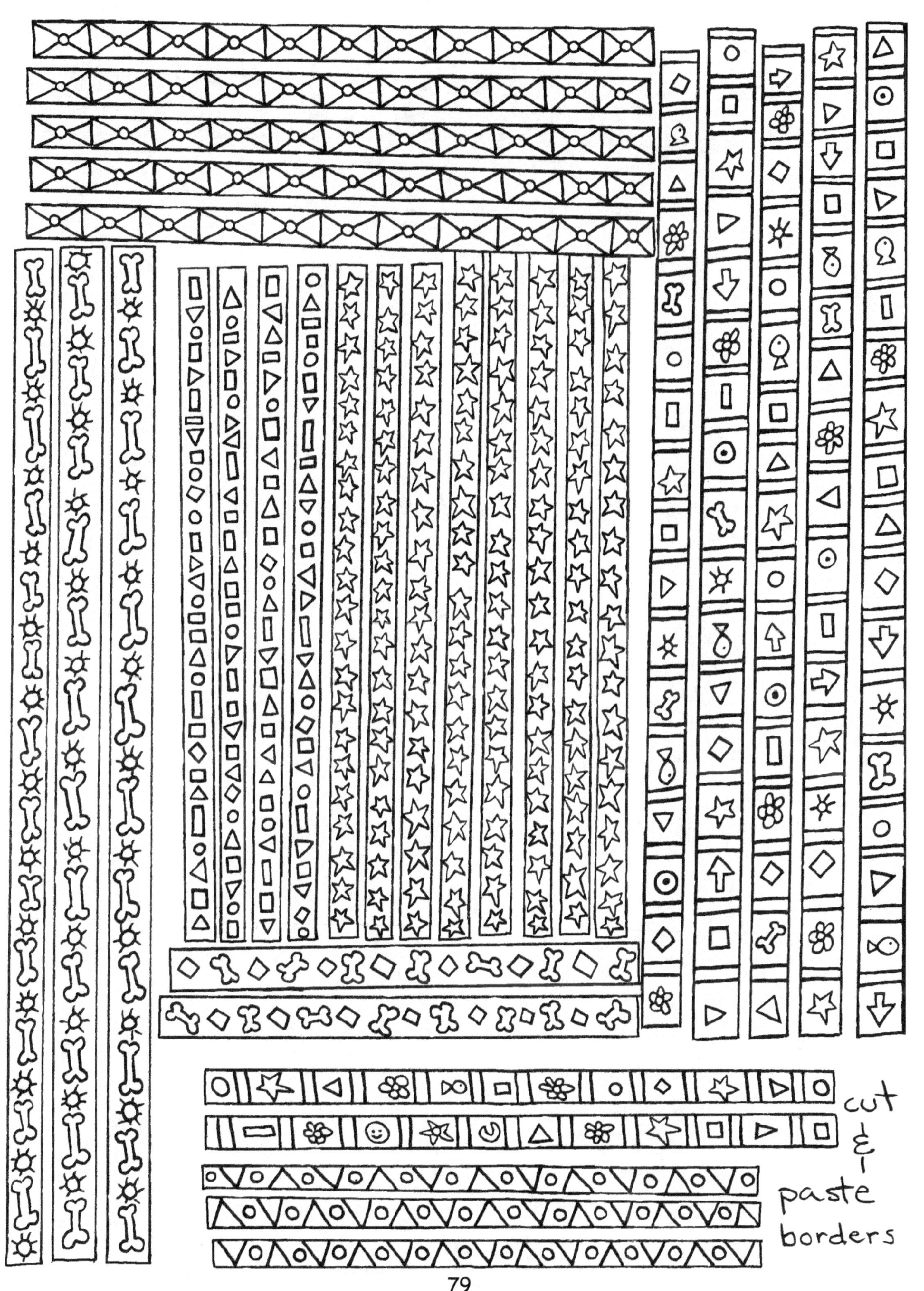

cut
&
paste
borders

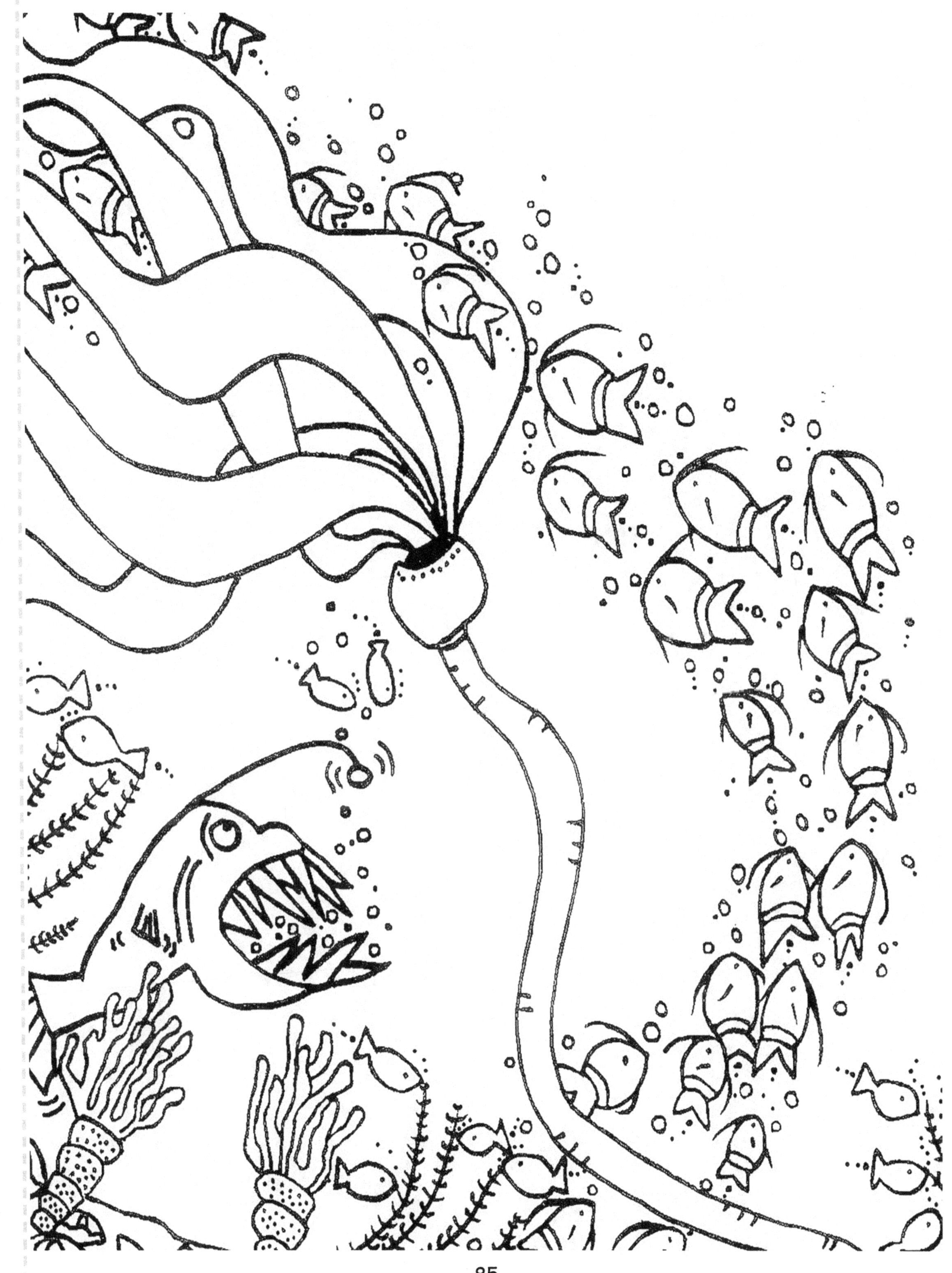

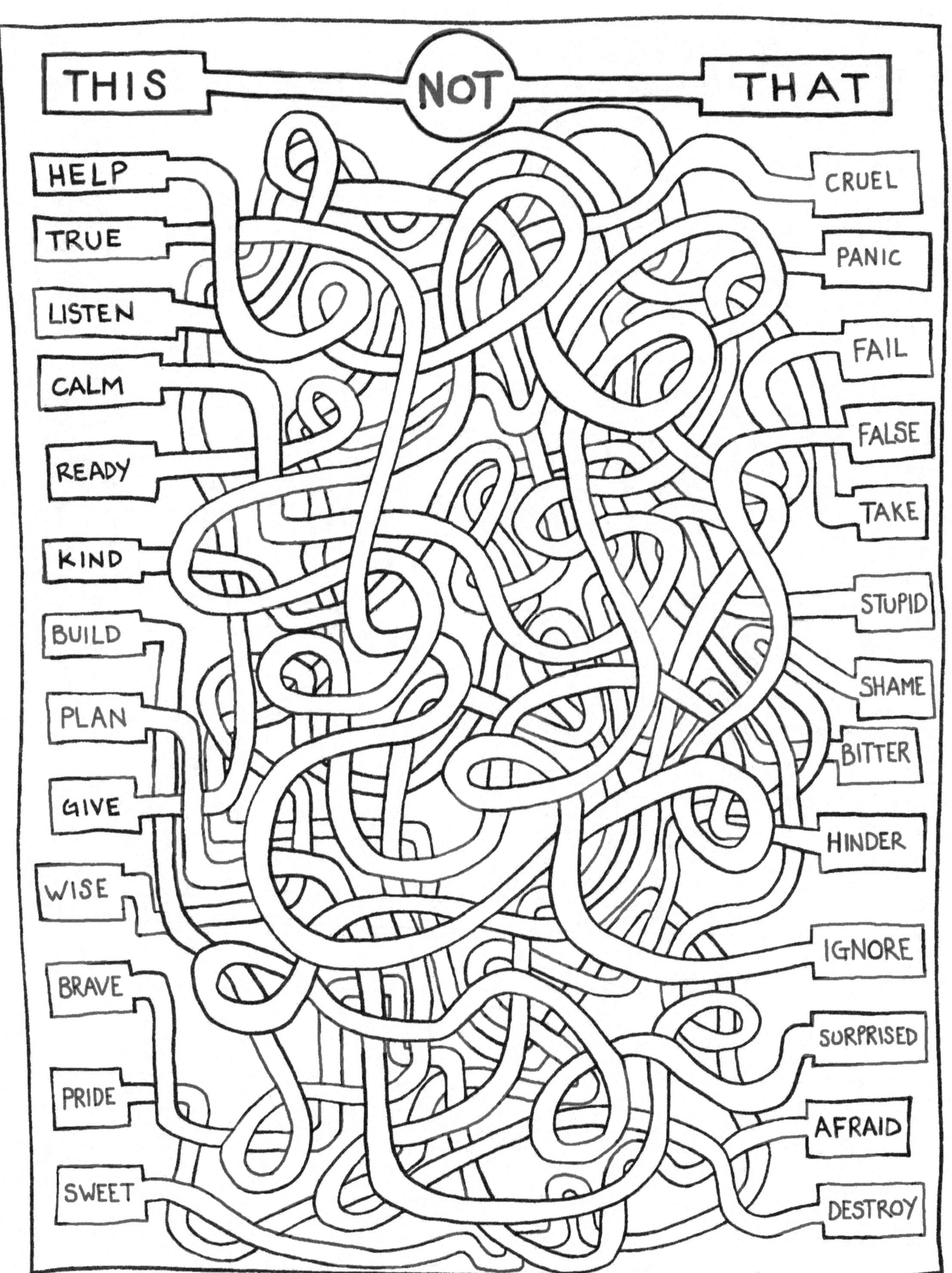

THIS
NOT
THAT
HELP
TRUE
LISTEN
CALM
READY
KIND
BUILD
PLAN
GIVE
WISE
BRAVE
PRIDE
SWEET
CRUEL
PANIC
FAIL
FALSE
TAKE
STUPID
SHAME
BITTER
HINDER
IGNORE
SURPRISED
AFRAID
DESTROY

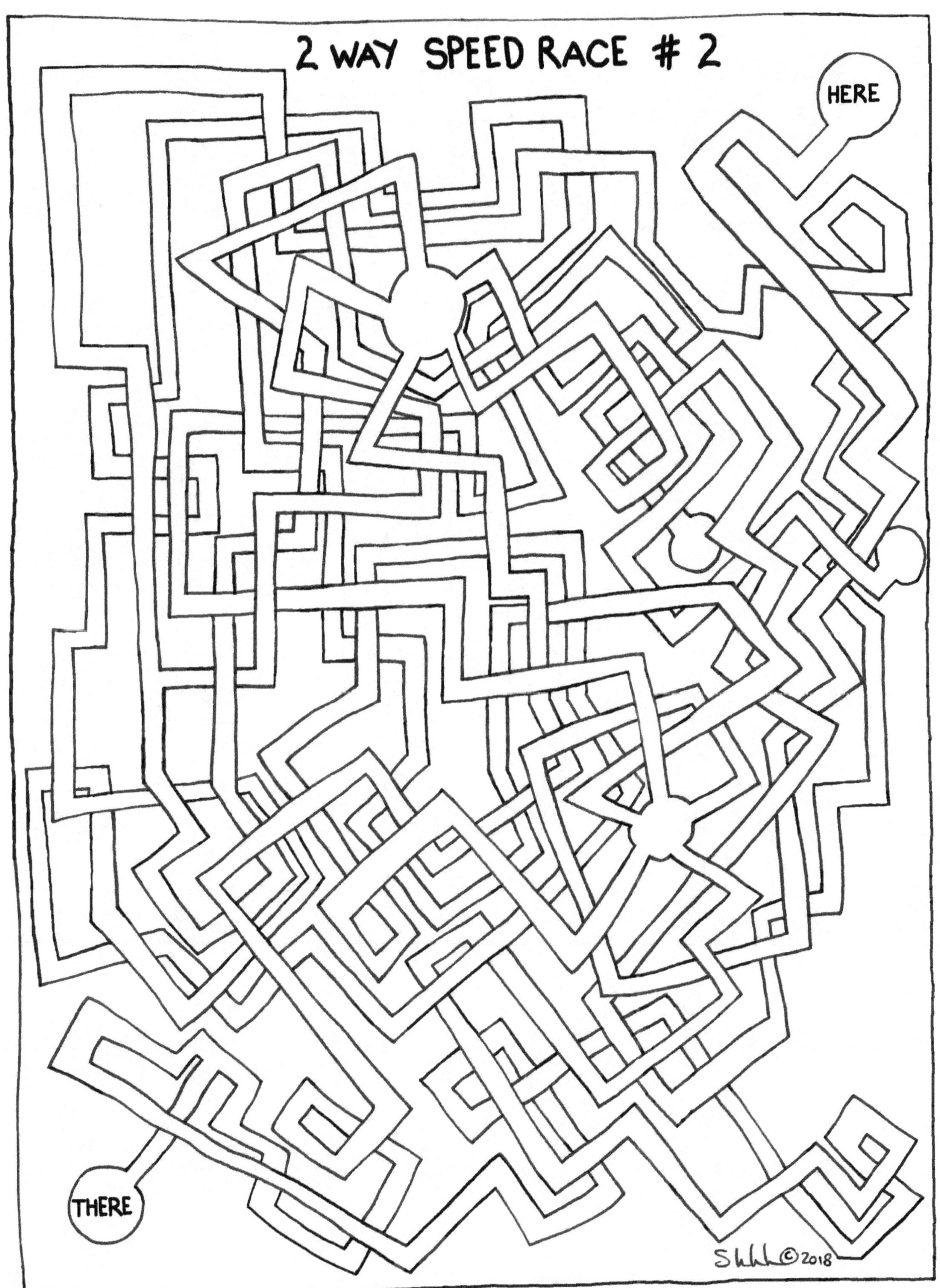

2 WAY SPEED RACE # 2
HERE
THERE
Shhh © 2018

COSMIC CAFE

```
S T R O P R A W E M I T A S K S S M
P R R U R N N L D N A P X E S G E A
R A I U S I O E N A M U H C U R E G
O N R S S H O G I E S S T B M A D N
P U E O K T M E T L R P R W N V I E
E L N C R S E E F A A O A V O I O T
L I A I R A L K H R T U E C L T R S
B L S N V E S S C O S N N E E Y T P
B T N C S E X S M O U O U G M M S L
U R I C I X R I M S R F L I H W A A
H O O O N X O S S E V I L A O L S N
S P R A N E O N E T P S E B R E T E
E E I T D C T T A S I S N M L V R T
D R O N E A S E E S A I A R A A E S
I S N E X P L O R E A O P R D R S A
T S N G I S A S T R O N A U G H T S
```

ALIEN	FISSION	NEON	SOLAR
ARORAS	FUEL	ORION	SPACE MAN
ASTROID	GEEKS	PANEL	SPACEX
ASTRONAUGHTS	GRASP	PLANS	STARS
BLACK HOLE	GRAVITY	PLANETS	STRESS
BLAST	HARSH	PORTS	TASKS
BUGS	HUBBLE	PROPEL	TEASE
COSMOS	HUMAN	RAINBOWS	TELESCOPE
CURE	INSANE	REPORT	TIDES
DARE	LAUNCH	RISKS	TIME WARP
DRONE	LIVES	ROCKETS	TOXICS
EARTH	LUNAR	ROOTS	TRAVEL
ECLIPSE	MAGNETS	RUSH	TRUST
ELON MUSK	MARS	SCRAP	UNIVERSE
EXIST	MOON	SEED	VENUS
EXPAND	MOTOR	SIGNS	
EXPLORE	NASA	SLIMY	

PEACE
MUSIC
SMILES
welcome
LIFE
honor
G
ART
LOVE
TIME
energy
MIND
i
CALM
NOW
Pride
Food
REAL
MAGIC
JOY
freedom
E
Tunes
OFTEN
99

so Sweet · Alone · WAY TO GO!

With You · to Love · Thank You

to be · Together · get well soon

WAITING · IN TIME · your Kindness

FUTURE · Your Smile

to the · for the · so much · such a

WAY 2 GO !!

THANK YOU · to me · for You

HAPPY BirthDAY · ENJOY

113

AT THE BEACH

```
E M G S N A E C A T S U R C S B L C
G R A N U L E S E T I K D R R I A R
S E U E I C S S N A T U E A M K S E
H T E S R N I U E O O E V B E I R A
E T R E A D I N A L B E M S S N E T
L E S O R E Y H C F T A V N L I F E
L B R K H U R A S I E S W A W A R E
S A G F Y S S T D R P H A E R I U F
D L O N G B E A C H A O O C O A S T
R L E T T E L E E L S R R O D S R E
I S A W F P C U E L Y E C Y D N I W
B L T E O I D S E S P L A S H Y A I
F I R O S T R R P P P I S S T V H S
S A L T Y U L D I E A N C R E A C H
B S N O S S E L E N H E I S C A R E
L D O O W T F I R D K D S K C A N S
```

BALLS	DRIFTWOOD	OCEAN	SOFT
BAREFEET	DRINK	ORCAS	SPEND
BEERS	EASE	PIER	SPLASH
BETTER	EELS	PLEASURE	STARS
BIRDS	FLAT	RAFT	SUNHAT
BIKINI	FLIPPER	RAVE	SURFERS
BRAVE	FLOAT	RODS	TANS
CAKES	FREE	SAILS	TIDAL POOLS
CHAIRS	FRISBE	SALTY	TOWELS
CLOUD	GRANULES	SANDCASTLES	TOYS
COAST	HAPPY	SCARE	TREASURE
CRABS	ICE CREAM	SHELLS	WAVES
CREATE	KITES	SHINING	WET FEET
CRUSTACEANS	LIFE	SHORELINE	WHALES
DAY DREAM	LIMB	SHORTS	WINDY
DIRTY	LESSONS	SKY BLUE	WISE
DRIFT	LONG BEACH	SNACKS	WISHES

2 Way Speed Race # 3

Thank you !!

To all who have helped me
with this book and to all who take
time to enjoy it.

It's been Amazing!!

Sheila Leigh Williams Sechelt, BC, Canada
whirledwidedesigns.com